Problem of the Week
Grade 6
A Fresh Approach to Problem-Solving

by Linda Griffin and Glenda DeMoss

illustrated by Randy Rider

cover illustration by Randy Rider

Publisher
Instructional Fair • TS Denison
Grand Rapids, Michigan 49544

TEACHING NOTES
★★★★★

Birthday Bonanza

NCTM Standards
- Problem Solving
- Reasoning
- Computation and Estimation
- Algebra

Possible Strategies
- Make a chart
- Use a spreadsheet
- Act it out

Suggested Materials
- Lined and unlined paper
- Calculator
- Computer spreadsheet

What to suggest if students are stuck

Use slips of paper to stand for "checks" from Aunt Isabella. Start with a $10 check. Next write a $30 check, then a $50 check. Continue in this way until the total of all the checks is $4,000.

Make a chart as shown. Keep track of the amount given each year and a running total of all the money she has sent. Continue the chart until the total amount is $4,000.

Birthday	Amt. This Year	Total
1	$10.00	$10.00
2	$30.00	$40.00
3	$50.00	$90.00
4	$70.00	$160.00
5	$90.00	$250.00

Make this chart on a spreadsheet. Type appropriate formulas to generate the amount this year and the total amount. Have the computer generate additional lines in the chart until you find a total of $4,000.

Complete solution

When you turn 20 years old, you will have received a total of $4,000.

Birthday	Amt. This Year	Total
1	$10.00	$10.00
2	$30.00	$40.00
3	$50.00	$90.00
4	$70.00	$160.00
5	$90.00	$250.00
6	$110.00	$360.00
7	$130.00	$490.00
8	$150.00	$640.00
9	$170.00	$810.00
10	$190.00	$1,000.00
11	$210.00	$1,210.00
12	$230.00	$1,440.00
13	$250.00	$1,690.00
14	$270.00	$1,960.00
15	$290.00	$2,250.00
16	$310.00	$2,560.00
17	$330.00	$2,890.00
18	$350.00	$3,240.00
19	$370.00	$3,610.00
20	$390.00	$4,000.00

ISBN: 1-56822-619-5
Problem of the Week—Grade 6
Copyright © 1998 by Instructional Fair • TS Denison
2400 Turner Avenue NW
Grand Rapids, Michigan 49544

Table of Contents

Foreword

The practice of assigning a Problem of the Week is well established in many classrooms, but it is difficult to manage such assignments at the middle school level in a way which promotes the development of successful problem-solving skills. The approach presented in this series has been used successfully by the authors in middle school classrooms for a number of years. This management scheme serves to foster confident problem solvers who exhibit the social skills necessary to function in a group and the ability to communicate mathematically. In these pages you will encounter motivating, challenging, and entertaining problems for your students. In addition, you will find a system for assigning these problems which can be readily implemented in your classroom. This approach will engage your students in the process of becoming skillful, capable, and confident problem solvers.

About This Series

The National Council of Teachers of Mathematics (NCTM) has made recommendations for the direction of mathematics education in its *Curriculum and Evaluation Standards*. In this document, "Mathematics as Problem Solving" is listed as the first instructional component for students at every grade level. The NCTM *Standards* suggests that students in grades five through eight have problem-solving opportunities in which they are encouraged to model problems concretely, to gather and organize data in tables, to identify patterns, and to use calculators to simplify computations. The series *Problem of the Week* 6, 7, 8 aligns with NCTM recommendations.

This series includes three books which contain problems appropriate for students in grades 6, 7, and 8. While each volume contains problems geared for an identified grade, teachers may find that problems from one of the other books in the series best suit the problem-solving ability of their students and should use the level or levels which fit best. Each book contains a description of this problem-solving approach, along with the answers to implementation questions which teachers frequently ask. The major portion of each book consists of 36 problems for students to solve. Each problem is accompanied by a facing "Teaching Notes" page which provides information about the mathematics involved in each problem, the problem-solving strategies which might apply, a list of suggested materials, several approaches that students might use to begin the problem, as well as a complete solution to the problem.

The problems are arranged in groups of three and are intended to be assigned as described in the list of features on page 2. The groupings are coded at the top of each "Teaching Notes" page as Set A, Set B, etc. The teacher who follows our problem-solving approach will have enough problems for an entire year of problem-solving assignments. Teachers who assign a problem a week will also find enough problems for the entire school year.

Fresh Approach Features

- A set of three problems is assigned every third week and is a required assignment for all students. Students are allowed one week to complete the problem set.

- Each set contains problems from a variety of strands which might be approached using several different problem-solving strategies.

- The problems are solved cooperatively in groups, but each individual student is responsible for turning in his/her complete set of solutions.

- All work towards solutions is done in class. The problems are not to be taken home.

- Students turn in a "write-up" which includes all work, answers, and a written explanation of the problem-solving method used to find the solution.

Questions and Answers About Implementation

Why assign problems in sets of three rather than one problem a week?

The goal in this approach is to have all students engaged in meaningful problem solving with their peers on a regular basis. Accomplishing this requires a substantial commitment of class time. While it may be unreasonable to fit problem-solving time into each week's lesson plans, it is not unmanageable to allot a block of class time for problem solving three times each quarter.

Allowing two weeks between each assigned set provides adequate time for the teacher to assess and respond to student work before assigning the next group of problems. Students have the opportunity to benefit from the comments made by the teacher, and their work may improve on the next assignment.

When problem solving is assigned less frequently, students respond positively to the change in routine. They may even look forward to problem-solving weeks! When problems are grouped, they form a substantial assignment which is difficult even for reluctant problem solvers to ignore.

Why should problems be required rather than extra credit?

The goal in assigning problem solving is to engage *all* students in the process. If a problem-solving assignment is optional as extra credit, the message is communicated to students that problem solving is not as important as other work done in class. If assigned as extra credit, it is almost impossible to ensure that students will work in groups to solve the problems.

Why are the problems grouped to represent a variety of mathematical strands?

It is effective to group the problems in each set to represent a variety of strands so that students gain the benefit of encountering problems in many mathematical areas throughout the school year. That is, in addition to a unit of study in an area like geometry or probability or number theory, students regularly encounter these topics through their problem-solving assignments. This process keeps a variety of mathematical topics in students' working repertoires.

Why are the problems grouped to represent different problem-solving strategies?

A situation is a "problem" if it requires the use of mathematical ideas and if the solution cannot be directly found using a rote process familiar to the student. When problems are grouped in a way that will allow all problems to be solved using a designated strategy, the problem-solving process can seem to be the rote application of that strategy. When students are regularly told which strategy applies to a certain problem, they are not being exposed to a complete problem-solving experience. The process of choosing a strategy is the integral first step in the solving of any problem.

It is also important to remember that every problem presented in this series can be solved in more than one way. It is misleading to students to suggest that a specific problem should be solved using a particular strategy.

Why do you have students work in groups rather than individually?

The NCTM *Standards* lists "Mathematics as Communication" as one of the four standards to be emphasized at all grade levels. In its description of this goal, the *Standards* recommends that students have many opportunities to use language to communicate their mathematical ideas through talking about their thinking and through written communication. This process helps to clarify students' ideas for themselves and gives the teacher valuable information about each student's mathematical understanding. Solving problems in groups provides a vehicle for this type of communication.

Additionally, there are mutual benefits for the student and the teacher when students are organized in small groups to solve problems. Students generally feel that stress is reduced when given the chance to work with peers. They have the opportunity to offer ideas and receive immediate feedback on those ideas. Groups maximize the opportunities students have for active participation in the problem-solving process.

When students work in groups, the teacher benefits as well. Students often request a great deal of assistance while working on problems. It is frustrating for the teacher to look around the classroom and see many hands raised, and students are likely to wait unproductively until the teacher can get to each of them. If they are expected to follow the group rules that are suggested, groups become somewhat self-sufficient. Students must ask their group members for help first. Often at least one member of the group can supply an answer or part of an answer which can keep the group on task. If all group members have a question, then the teacher can assist the entire group by clarifying the task or suggesting a way to proceed. This strategy enables the teacher to interact with seven or eight groups rather than 28 or 32 individuals.

What group rules are successful?

The group rules listed below work well with students engaged in problem-solving assignments. These rules come from a variety of sources and have been modified to suit this classroom environment.

GROUP RULES

1. Use the first names of the people in your group.
2. All group members must be working on the same problem at the same time.
3. Ask a group member for help when needed. Give help to group members when asked.
4. Ask the teacher for help only if all group members have the same question.
5. Only one person may leave your group at a time.

There are many good books and articles devoted to the use of cooperative learning and how to make this teaching strategy work in the math classroom. A few good resources we recommend follow.

Johnson, David W., Johnson, Roger T. and Holubec, Edythe Johnson. *Cooperation in the Classroom.* Interaction Book Co., 1988.

Erickson, Tim. *Get It Together*: *Math Problems for Groups, Grades 4-12.* Lawrence Hall of Science, 1989.

Davidson, Neil, ed. *Cooperative Learning in Mathematics.* Addison-Wesley, 1996.

What is the rationale for group rules?

The guiding principle here is to get students to work together and to interact with mathematical ideas. All of the rules support this idea. Rule #1 requiring the use of names promotes positive social interaction. Requiring that students work on the same problem at the same time (rule #2) is the key to the group process. The benefits of working together are undermined if students divide the work and then share solutions. Rules #3 and #4 require that students rely on one another for help rather than the teacher as much as possible, which helps foster habits of independent learning. Rule #5 is a wonderful management tool. Allowing only one person to leave the group at a time ensures that a group of students stays together while working on problems. As a result, the amount of movement and confusion in the classroom is kept to a minimum.

FOLLOW THE RULES, SOLVE THE PROBLEM. WHAT A SYSTEM!

What should the teacher do if a group is stuck and asks for help?

Each "Teaching Notes" page offers a wide variety of strategies that can be used by students. Rather than providing answers, the teacher can suggest these strategies and approaches or can model a process that might be useful. Experience suggests that when helping students, the more writing the teacher does, the less useful that information is to confused students. A rule of thumb when helping a group is to have students, *not the teacher*, holding their pencils.

What if a group is unproductive? How do you get students back on track?

Whatever regular system is in place in the classroom for productive work time should be applied. In addition, a system that has proven to be successful is the inclusion of "group points" in the final grade on the problem-solving assignment. Ten or fifteen percent of the problem-solving grade can be allotted as group points. Each group begins the week with all of its group points but loses one point each time the teacher notices that group members are not following the group rules. Following this system, groups tend to monitor themselves.

Another way to handle unproductive groups is to remove the unproductive member (or members) and require that student to work individually. This sends the message that the opportunity to work in a group is a privilege which must be earned. Most middle school students prefer to work with others rather than by themselves on assignments as involved as problem solving, and they will strive to behave accordingly. Be certain to guard against regularly taking away the group structure for certain students. The intent of the problem-solving assignment is to create a situation in which students work *with their peers*.

If students work together in groups, why should each individual turn in his/her own work?

Individual accountability is the main concern. It is tempting for some students when assigned to a group to let others do much of the work. Since everyone has to turn in his/her work, every student must attend to the task of solving the problems. Even if one member of the group takes the lead in solving a problem, all group members must communicate about the task to demonstrate understanding of the process used to solve it.

In addition, the fact that students are working in groups does not mean each member of the group is using the same strategy or thinking about the solution in the same way. It is possible that students in the same group may not even agree on a solution, which is perfectly acceptable. Each student should, however, be able to defend the method used and justify the solution in his/her write-up.

Why not assign problem solving as homework?

When problem solving is assigned to be done at home, it often fails to be a meaningful experience for students. Problem solving is most productive when the problem solver is able to work with a peer. Parents do not fill that role. Quite often what happens is that "helpful" parents give answers rather than productive help. It is not uncommon for problem-solving assignments which are sent home to be turned in by students using formulas and/or methods which are quite meaningless to the student.

Other parents may be uncomfortable when "hard" problems come home. Such parents may complain that the assignment is unfair or inappropriate for their child. It may be difficult for parents to understand that an algebra problem could be assigned to students who are not studying algebra, the intent being to encourage students to solve the problem by using a strategy such as logical reasoning, making a table, or looking for a pattern.

If students are to follow group rule #2 (all group members must be working on the same problem at the same time), taking work home is counterproductive. If a student does not bring work back the next day, that student cannot participate productively with the group. If a student works on a problem at home and other group members do not, that student gets "ahead" of the group and is no longer a productive group member.

What are the advantages to having students work on problems in class and not at home?

There are three aspects to consider. The first is time. Middle school students working on problems outside of class often spend as little time as possible working towards a solution. When class time is devoted to problem solving, all students have the opportunity to dedicate a significant amount of time to each assignment.

The second consideration is the opportunity to work with peers. The problem-solving process is greatly enhanced when students are required to work with their peers. Ideas and strategies can be shared and compared when students work with their classmates. In the classroom, the teacher has the opportunity to establish rules and procedures that support productive peer interaction.

The third reason for devoting class time to problem solving is that in class students have access to positive guidance from the teacher. Rather than providing answers, the teacher can suggest strategies and approaches by giving hints or by modeling processes that might be useful. This is not the kind of help students generally receive from their parents at home.

What suggestions do you have for managing student work in the classroom if it cannot be taken home?

Making use of group folders works well in the classroom. Each group can have a folder in which all work is placed at the end of the class period. Each student should label all work and staple or paper clip individual papers together. At the beginning of a problem-solving period, one group member gets the group folder with everyone's work. At the end of a problem-solving period, one group member collects the work in the folder and replaces it in the file box or drawer.

Would you ever allow students to take their problems home?

If problems are assigned on Monday and due the following Monday, students can be allowed to take their work home over the weekend to prepare the problem-solving sets for submission for a grade. This should only be an option if the student has already solved each problem or is clearly on the road to a solution.

How much class time should be set aside for problem solving?

Since problems are assigned every third week rather than one each week, a substantial amount of classroom time should be dedicated to students working on problems together in groups. Middle school students should be allowed the equivalent of two class periods, or roughly 90 minutes, in a problem-solving week to work exclusively on the problem set.

It is important that problem-solving time be spread throughout the week to provide students with enough time to ponder and gain new insights into problems. Many scheduling schemes are possible. Three examples are listed below:

1. Monday—30 minutes; Tuesday, Wednesday, Thursday, and Friday—15 minutes each
2. Monday and Tuesday—45 minutes each with problem solving as an option during regularly scheduled independent work time the rest of the week
3. Monday—45 minutes; Tuesday and Thursday—20 to 25 minutes each

How do I use the other classroom minutes during a problem-solving week?

While solving nonroutine problems is a worthwhile activity, it is important that it not usurp all the class time during a week in which they are assigned. Attention to the rest of the curriculum should be maintained. Problem-solving assignments should serve to enhance the mathematical experience for students. Teachers should proceed with lessons in the unit or about the topic that students are studying at the time. Since problems are not to be taken home, it is perfectly appropriate to assign regular daily homework to accompany these lessons.

How can I compensate for "lost" time during a problem-solving week?

There is no easy answer to this question. Teachers who are committed to providing a quality problem-solving experience for students must efficiently use *all* class time. Streamlining such tasks as homework correction and collection, attendance procedures, and classroom routines for getting started and cleaning up add minutes to each class period which have a cumulative effect on instructional time. Some good resources for ideas on this topic are

Purdy, Scott. *Time Management for Teachers*. Write Time, 1995.
Johnson David R. *Every Minute Counts: Making Your Math Class Work*. Dale Seymour Publications, 1982.
Johnson, David R. *Making Minutes Count Even More*. Dale Seymour Publications, 1986.

In addition, keep in mind that the time is not "lost" when students work on problem sets. Students are gaining experience in the content areas while engaged in problem solving. As a result, students become better thinkers and better mathematicians, which allows the teaching of the other portion of the curriculum to be more productive.

Why should students be required to produce a "lab-type" write-up?

The writing required is a logical extension of the group process for problem solving. Students communicate verbally with their peers while working with their groups and then formalize this thinking in a write-up. Writing should be a part of learning in every subject area, and mathematics is no exception.

Communication is crucial to students' mathematical understanding. Problem solvers who do not develop communication skills will find they have difficulty applying their skills in real life situations.

What should be included in a student's write-up?

Having read the write-up, the reader should be able to use the writer's strategies and logic to solve the indicated problem. It should include a step-by-step account of the writer's process along with any dead-ends or false starts. Pictures, charts, and diagrams might accompany the writing to clarify or illustrate patterns and generalizations which led to the solution. For examples, see pages 13 and 14.

How do you get students to write complete explanations about problem solving?

Modeling is the most effective strategy to use with students in this area. The first time a set of problems is assigned, students should solve them with their groups but work together as a class under the teacher's direction when they compose a write-up. Students share their strategies and logic with the class while the teacher records what is being said on the overhead projector or chalkboard. The teacher's writing can be edited by the class; then each student can record it on his/her paper. This procedure could be repeated for some, but not all, of the problems in the next few sets until students are able to proceed independently.

There are many good books about writing in the math class. One of them is
  Burns, Marilyn. *Writing in Math Class: A Resource for Grades 2-8.* Burns Education Assocs., 1995.

How do calculators fit with problem solving?

Calculators should be available for students at all times when engaged in problem solving. The NCTM recommends that all students have a calculator with functions consistent with the tasks outlined in the *Standards*. For this reason, calculators are listed as a suggested material on each "Teaching Notes" page. All of the problems in this series can be solved using a four-function calculator, but students may find a scientific calculator useful at times.

How do computers fit with problem solving?

A computer spreadsheet is a powerful problem-solving tool. The "Teaching Notes" pages refer to its use when appropriate and include suggestions for setting up charts using a spreadsheet. It is not the intent of this series to teach students how to use a spreadsheet. The assumption has been made that in classrooms equipped with this technology, students have a working knowledge of spreadsheet use.

Keep in mind that a spreadsheet is *not* required to solve any problem in the series.

What classroom features promote success in problem solving?

Desks or chairs should be arranged so that students in a group can communicate and share materials easily while working on problems. Several common classroom items should be available for student use in addition to the calculator. These include scissors, tape, graph paper, counters, and rulers. Student creativity in solving problems is greatly enhanced when a variety of supplies is readily accessible.

What grading system supports productive problem solving?

The grading system used to assess problem-solving assignments should reflect the value placed on the process of finding an answer, not simply on the correct answer itself. A grading system for problem-solving assignments should place about 40 percent of its weight on the correctness of the answer and about 60 percent of its weight on explanations that completely describe the process or method used to arrive at the student's solution. With this weighting of grades, students will quickly see that it is impossible to get a passing grade on the problem-solving set without providing complete explanations, even if students' answers are correct. Likewise, it is theoretically possible to get a passing grade on a set of problems even if all of a student's answers are incorrect, provided the student explains completely how he or she arrived at those answers.

Reluctant problem solvers often find comfort in this grading system since it seems to remove the pressure to find the "right" answer. Middle school students are generally willing to take more risks in problem solving when their level of grade anxiety has been reduced in this way.

How should points be assigned in a grading system like this?

One way of grading problem sets is to make them worth 30 points each. Each problem is worth 10 points, 4 points for the correct answer and 6 points for a complete explanation. Within this structure, each problem would be graded according to the rubric below.

The four points assigned to the answer could be awarded as follows:

0 points	Student does not submit an answer.
1 point	Student provides an incorrect and unreasonable answer.
2 - 3 points	Student provides an incorrect but reasonable answer.
4 points	Student provides a complete, correct answer.

The six points assigned to the explanation could be awarded as follows:

0 points	Student writes no explanation and shows little or no work.
1 - 2 points	Student shows all work but does not write an explanation of his/her strategy.
3 - 5 points	Student shows all work and includes an explanation which lacks one or more key components.
6 points	Student shows all work and writes a complete step-by-step explanation of strategies used to solve the problem, which the reader can easily follow to understand the solution.

What should I expect student work to look like? That is, what does a "10" paper look like?

The grading of the problem-solving sets is a subjective process, but it is important to standardize the teacher's expectations and clearly communicate these to students. Following are examples of graded student work on the "Bean Bags" problem in the sixth grade book from this series.

Bean Bags

Lima beans come in 3-pound and 5-pound bags which cost $1.15 and $1.63 respectively. How many of each should you buy to have at least 17 pounds of lima beans at the lowest cost?

Student #1

First I read the problem and noticed that I do not have to buy exactly 17 pounds. I could buy more if that is cheaper. I decided to make a chart to compare all the ways I could get at least 17 pounds. In my chart I started with all 3-pound bags, then some 3s with a 5, and continue until I had a combination with all 5s. By doing this, I was sure I would not miss any possible combinations. Here is my chart. I marked the answer with an arrow.

Grade/Comments:

+ 4   correct answer

+ 6   Your logic and strategy are easy to follow. The chart is very clear and systematic.

Score: 10/10

3-pound Bags	5-pound Bags	Total Pounds	Total Cost
6	0	18	$6.90
5	1	20	$7.38
4	1	17	$6.23
3	2	19	$6.71
2	3	21	$7.19
1	3	18	$6.04	←
0	4	20	$6.52

Student #2

3 + 5 + 5 + 5 = 18   too much
3 + 3 + 5 + 5 = 16   not enough
3 + 3 + 3 + 5 + 5 = 19   too much
3 + 3 + 3 + 3 + 5 = 17   this is it!

4 of the 3-pound bags: 4 x $1.15 = $4.60
1 of the 5-pound bags: 1 x $1.63 = $1.63
                      TOTAL = $6.23

I tried to find combinations of 5 and 3 that made 17. The only one I found was 3 + 3 + 3 + 3 + 5. The cost for this was $6.23. I know this works because I tried it.

Grade/Comments:

+ 2   There is a cheaper way!

+ 5   You did a good job of explaining what you did. Your systematic list is very clear, but the problem says you need *at least* 17 pounds . . . you can buy more than 17 pounds.

Score: 7/10

Student #3		Grade/Comments:
1.15 ÷ 3= .3833333	1.63 ÷ 5 =.326	+ 4 correct answer
4 x 5 = 20 pounds (3 x 5) + (1 x 3) = 18 pounds	4 x 1.63 = $6.52 (3 x 1.63) + 1.15 = $6.04	+ 4 Finding the unit was a good way to start. I wonder how you can be certain there isn't another combination of bags that gives a better price. Either explain your logic or show other combinations you could try.

First I found the price per pound for each bag. The 5-pound bag is the cheapest per pound, so I want to buy mostly those. I found that four of the 5-pound bags gave me 20 pounds for $6.60. I tried using three of the 5-pound bags with one 3-pound bag and found that I had more than 17 pounds, but it cost less. This is the best combination.

Score: 8/10

How do group points fit into this grading scheme?

Another five points can come from the group points given to each group at the beginning of the problem-solving week. If all of the members follow the group rules during the time allotted in the classroom to work on the problems, they each keep the five points. Points are taken away from each group member every time the teacher notices a group member is not following a group rule. The remaining group points are then added to the points from each student's write-up for a total score out of 35 points.

How much weight should a problem-solving assignment have towards a student's final grade?

The problem set should be worth enough to significantly impact the grade of a student who repeatedly fails to turn them in. They should not, however, be weighted so heavily that students feel great pressure to get all the points on every problem. It is reasonable to assign weight to each set of problems roughly the same as one quiz grade. Weighting the assignment in this manner communicates to students that problem solving is as important as other aspects of their mathematics curriculum.

How do I establish a positive classroom climate which promotes problem solving?

It is the teacher who establishes a classroom climate for problem solving. From the first day of the school year, students notice subtle messages from the teacher which impact the way they will react to a problem-solving assignment. A classroom in which students are encouraged to be essentially self-sufficient and independent thinkers is a classroom more conducive to successful problem solving.

A classroom which promotes problem solving is one in which the teacher asks thought-provoking questions and listens to many thoughtful student responses. Whether introducing problems to be solved or providing explanations for the lesson of the day, the teacher who asks for student responses, waits to give time for students to think, then calls on students to provide answers which require an explanation, is setting a tone in the classroom which values students' thinking. By routinely asking good questions which require more than a yes/no response, the teacher gives students the opportunity to practice the kind of thinking required of them in a problem-solving assignment. The teacher's response to student answers is important as well. If incorrect or unconventional responses are dismissed by the teacher in a manner which demeans the student, it is unlikely that students will feel free to suggest or try novel thinking when asked to do so on a problem-solving assignment.

Students should be encouraged to turn to one another for help before seeking help from the teacher. The teacher should foster peer interaction by regularly directing students to other students for help. Additionally, the teacher communicates the value of student thinking by listening attentively to student responses and by expecting students to do the same with their peers.

Students should believe that there are many "right ways" to solve a problem and that every problem can be approached in a variety of ways. The teacher must create this atmosphere by modeling many approaches to problems and by accepting student-suggested methods.

TEACHING NOTES
★★★★★

Which Order?

NCTM Standards
- Problem Solving
- Reasoning

Possible Strategies
- Eliminate possibilities
- Make a model
- Draw a picture
- Guess and check

Suggested Materials
- Lined and unlined paper
- Calculator

What to suggest if students are stuck

Cut five slips of paper and label each with a name of a student. Place them in any order; then check this arrangement against the information in the problem. If your arrangement does not work, rearrange and try again.

Draw five squares to represent the five desks in a row. Fill in the names in places which can be determined directly from clues. Now place the others at random and see whether they fit all the remaining clues. If your arrangement does not work, rearrange and try again.

Complete solution

They are seated as shown below:

front | Blake | Charles | Emily | Audrey | Diane |

Which Order?

Audrey, Blake, Charles, Diane, and Emily sit in the same row of desks in math class. The two boys sit one after the other. Diane, the tallest, is in the last seat. Charles sits right in front of his twin sister. Audrey sits in between the other two girls. In which order are the five students sitting? _____

_____

TEACHING NOTES
★★★★

Mr. Macho's Appetite

NCTM Standards
- Problem Solving
- Reasoning
- Computation and Estimation
- Algebra

Possible Strategies
- Guess and check
- Look for a pattern
- Make a chart
- Use a spreadsheet

Suggested Materials
- Lined and unlined paper
- Calculator
- Computer spreadsheet

What to suggest if students are stuck

Make a chart to show the five days. Guess the amount he might have eaten on the first day. Repeatedly increase this amount by seven to get the amount eaten on each of the next four days. Find the total. If the total is not 125, adjust your guess based on the information from the previous guess.

Monday	Tuesday	Wednesday	Thursday	Friday	Total
7	14	21	28	35	105
8	15	22	29	36	110

Look for a pattern as you adjust each guess. How does changing the number eaten on the first day by one affect the total?

Make this chart on a spreadsheet. Fill in the appropriate formulas for finding the amount eaten each day (M, T, W, Th, F) and for the total. Enter guesses for the first day. Continue guessing until the total is 125.

Complete solution

He ate 11 hot dogs the first day.

Monday	Tuesday	Wednesday	Thursday	Friday	Total
7	14	21	28	35	105
8	15	22	29	36	110
9	16	23	30	37	115
10	17	24	31	38	120
11	18	25	32	39	125

Name _____

Mr. Macho's Appetite

Mr. Macho, my great dane, ate 125 hot dogs over a five-day period. Each day he ate seven more hot dogs than on the previous day. How many hot dogs did he eat on the first day? _____

_____

TEACHING NOTES
★★★★★

Garden Plots

NCTM Standards
- Problem Solving
- Reasoning
- Computation and Estimation
- Patterns and Functions
- Geometry
- Algebra

Possible Strategies
- Draw a picture
- Make a list
- Guess and check

Suggested Materials
- Lined and unlined paper
- Calculator
- Graph paper

What to suggest if students are stuck

Outline a rectangle which has an area of 60 on graph paper. Adjust this rectangle by making it one foot wider and three feet shorter. See whether the area of the new rectangle equals 60.

Make a list of all the possible (whole number) starting dimensions the rectangle could have had. Find a pair of dimensions which has the same relationship that is described in the problem.

Complete solution

Last year the garden plot was 4 feet x 15 feet. This year it is 5 feet x 12 feet.

Possible Sizes
1 x 60
2 x 30
3 x 20
4 x 15
5 x 12
6 x 10

One foot wider and three feet shorter

Garden Plots

Gloria had a rectangular garden plot last year with an area of 60 square feet. This year Gloria's garden plot is one foot wider and three feet shorter than last year's garden, but it has the same area. What were the dimensions of the garden last year? _____

TEACHING NOTES
★ ★ ★ ★

Hexagonal Doodles

NCTM Standards
- Problem Solving
- Reasoning
- Computation and Estimation
- Patterns and Functions
- Algebra
- Geometry

Possible Strategies
- Make a chart
- Look for a pattern
- Use a spreadsheet

Suggested Materials
- Lined and unlined paper
- Calculator
- Computer spreadsheet

What to suggest if students are stuck

Make a chart like the one shown. Count to determine the total number of dots after each new hexagon is drawn. Place this information in the chart. Look for a pattern to predict the total number of dots as another hexagon is added. Use this pattern to continue the chart until you reach the fiftieth entry.

# of Hexagons	Total # of Dots
1	6
2	11
3	16

Create this chart on a spreadsheet. Once you have identified the pattern for the total number of dots column, enter it as a formula so that the computer can complete the table to the fiftieth entry.

Find a relationship between the number in the first column and the number in the second column. If you can identify this relationship, you will not need to complete the chart.

Complete solution

There will be 251 dots after drawing 50 hexagons.

The relationship between # of hexagons and # of dots is this:
total number of dots = [(number of hexagons) x 5] + 1

The total number of dots after 50 hexagons is 50 x 5 + 1 = 251.

Hexagonal Doodles

Oh brother! I am so bored! Mr. Blather, my science teacher, is lecturing on the weather patterns in the Arctic Circle. YAWN! YAWN! To keep myself awake, I started doodling. I started with one hexagon, then kept drawing larger and larger hexagons. I must be really bored because I found myself wondering how many dots I would have altogether after the fiftieth hexagon. What's the answer?

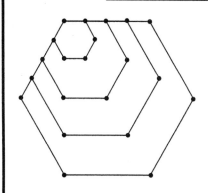

IN THE ARCTIC CIRCLE THE WEATHER IS REALLY, REALLY COLD. I'M NOT KIDDING.

Birthday Bonanza

Your eccentric Aunt Isabella sends money to each niece and nephew on his or her birthday. She gives each child $10 on his or her first birthday. On each birthday thereafter, you and your cousins get $20 more than on the birthday before. How old will you be when you have received a total of $4,000 from Aunt Isabella? _____

NOTHING SAYS, 'I LOVE YOU' LIKE COLD, HARD CASH!

Set B Problem 3

TEACHING NOTES
★★★★

Who's Married to Whom?

NCTM Standards
- Problem Solving
- Reasoning

Possible Strategies
- Act it out
- Eliminate possibilities
- Guess and check

Suggested Materials
- Lined and unlined paper
- Calculator
- Graph paper

What to suggest if students are stuck

Write the names of the eight people on slips of paper. Place the women together with the men in any combination. Check this arrangement with the clues in the problem. If it is not correct, make different pairings and try the clues again.

Use a matrix to keep track of the information. Place an X in any cell which cannot form a "couple." Do this until each woman is paired with her husband.

	Linda	Lisa	Glenda	Dee
Tom				
Duane			X	
Ron				
Ernie			X	

Complete solution

The couples are Linda and Ron, Lisa and Ernie, Glenda and Tom, and Dee and Duane.

	Linda	Lisa	Glenda	Dee
Tom	X	X	•	X
Duane	X	X	X	•
Ron	•	X	X	X
Ernie	X	•	X	X

Who's Married to Whom?

Four married couples belong to a club. The hostess posed this puzzle at the first meeting so that the members could figure out who was married to whom. She gave these clues to the group:

• The wives' names are Linda, Lisa, Glenda, and Dee.

• The husbands' names are Tom, Duane, Ron, and Ernie.

• Ernie is Glenda's brother.

• Glenda and Duane were once engaged, but "broke up" when Duane met his present wife.

• Dee has two brothers, but her husband is an only child.

• Linda is married to Ron.

So, who is married to whom? _____

_____

_____

I'D LIKE YOU TO MEET MY BETTER HALF— JUST AS SOON AS I FIGURE OUT WHO SHE IS.

TEACHING NOTES
★★★★

No Fours or Fives

NCTM Standards
- Problem Solving
- Reasoning
- Patterns and Functions

Possible Strategies
- Make a list
- Look for a pattern
- Eliminate possibilities

Suggested Materials
- Lined and unlined paper
- Calculator

What to suggest if students are stuck

Make an organized list. Start with numbers in the 10s. Which ones are possible? Next do the 20s, etc.

Look for a pattern in this list which will allow you to save time. How many numbers can be made in each decade? Which decades will be impossible? Use this information to determine how many numbers are possible.

List all the two-digit numbers (10 - 99). Cross out all the ones which have a 4 or a 5 or both. Count how many are left after these have been eliminated.

Complete solution

There are 56 numbers that fit this description.

There are seven possible decades (10s, 20s, 30s, 60s, 70s, 80s, 90s) each with eight numbers. This gives 7 x 8 = 56 numbers.

Tens	Twenties	Thirties	Sixties	Seventies	Eighties	Nineties
10	20	30	60	70	80	90
11	21	31	61	71	81	91
12	22	32	62	72	82	92
13	23	33	63	73	83	93
16	26	36	66	76	86	96
17	27	37	67	77	87	97
18	28	38	68	78	88	98
19	29	39	69	79	89	99

No Fours or Fives

Using the digits one through nine, how many two-digit numbers can be formed which *do not* contain a four or a five? _____

LET'S SEE...
THERE'S, UH,
LIKE...Y'KNOW...

TEACHING NOTES
★★★★★

By Leaps and Bounds

NCTM Standards
- Problem Solving
- Reasoning
- Number Theory
- Computation and Estimation
- Patterns and Functions
- Algebra

Possible Strategies
- Draw a picture
- Act it out
- Make a chart
- Look for a pattern
- Use a spreadsheet

Suggested Materials
- Lined and unlined paper
- Calculator
- Counters
- Meter stick or cm ruler

What to suggest if students are stuck

Cut a sheet of paper into strips and tape them together to represent the racetrack. (Let 1 cm = 1 step.) Place counters on the track in the correct position to represent the coyote and the rabbit. Move them according to the problem; that is, each time the coyote moves 14 steps, the rabbit moves 9 steps. Find the place where they meet.

Make a chart as shown. Since Joe is 60 steps ahead, start with Cunning Coyote at 0 and Joe Jackrabbit at 60. Increase each as stated in the problem; that is, add 14 to the coyote each time you add 9 to the rabbit. Find the point where they meet.

Coyote	Jackrabbit
0	60
14	69
28	78

Consider the "head start" (60) and the amount the coyote "gains" (14 - 9 = 5) in each time period. How many time periods would pass before the coyote made up the head start? (60 ÷ 5 = 12) How many steps would each runner take in that amount of time?

Complete solution

Cunning Coyote took 168 steps and Jackrabbit took 108 steps (168 - 60).

Coyote	Jackrabbit
0	60
14	69
28	78
42	87
56	96
70	105
84	114
98	123
112	132
126	141
140	150
154	159
168	168

By Leaps and Bounds

Cunning Coyote is in a race with Joe Jackrabbit. They both take the same size steps, but the coyote takes 14 steps in the time it takes the rabbit to take 9 steps. Cunning Coyote decided to let Joe get 60 steps ahead before he to started to run. How many steps will each runner take (from the time the coyote started running) before the coyote catches up to the rabbit? _____

TEACHING NOTES
★★★★
The Camp Cook

NCTM Standards
- Problem Solving
- Reasoning
- Number Theory
- Computation and Estimation
- Measurement

Possible Strategies
- Act it out
- Make a chart
- Draw a picture
- Use logical reasoning

Suggested Materials
- Lined and unlined paper
- Calculator
- Counters
- Paper plates or bags

What to suggest if students are stuck

Act it out using counters to stand for cups of milk. Start with a big supply of counters. Use three paper plates or bags to stand for the containers. Assume that you are filling each one by placing the indicated number of counters in each. Try "pouring" from one container to another until you have 17 cups of milk.

Draw a picture of the containers and make a chart to keep track of the amount of milk in the cooking pot.

5-gallon jug

7 cups   4 cups   cooking pot

7-cup Container	4-cup Container	Cooking Pot
0	0	0
7	0	0
3	4	0

Complete solution

Follow the steps indicated in the chart:

7-cup Container	4-cup Container	Cooking Pot
0	0	0
7	0	0
3	4	0
0	4	3
0	0	3	← return 4 cups to 5-gal. jug
7	0	0
0	0	10
7	0	10
0	0	17

The Camp Cook

Chester, the camp cook, has a problem. He forgot to bring his measuring cups with him on the camp out. He promised the campers he would make his famous Chocoblast Cocoa for the campfire sing-a-long. The recipe calls for 17 cups of milk. He has a 5-gallon jug that is almost full of milk. He also has an empty cooking pot and two (empty) small jugs, one that holds 4 cups and another one that holds 7 cups. Show how Chester can use the tools he has to measure *exactly* 17 cups of milk without wasting any milk. _____

_____

_____

_____

TEACHING NOTES
★ ★ ★ ★ ★

Off and On

NCTM Standards
- Problem Solving
- Reasoning
- Patterns and Functions

Possible Strategies
- Draw a picture
- Make a list
- Eliminate possibilities

Suggested Materials
- Lined and unlined paper
- Calculator
- Counters

What to suggest if students are stuck

Take out counters in two colors: one color for *on*, another for *off*. Arrange the counters to fit the restriction that no two adjacent switches can be off. Keep track of all the arrangements you find.

Make a list of the possible arrangements. Let X = off and O = on. Do this systematically to make certain you find all of them. Start with all switches on. Next arrange four on and one off. Continue systematically until you have found all the ways.

Make a list of all the ways the switches could be arranged without regard to the restriction listed in the problem. Now eliminate the arrangements in your list with two adjacent switches off.

Complete solution

There are 12 ways the switches can be arranged.

O	O	O	O	O
O	O	O	O	X
O	O	O	X	O
O	O	X	O	O
O	X	O	O	O
X	O	O	O	O
X	O	X	O	O
O	X	O	X	O
O	O	X	O	X
X	O	O	X	O
O	X	O	O	X
X	O	O	O	X

Name _____

Off and On

In how many different ways can a panel of five on-off switches be set if no two adjacent switches can be off? _____

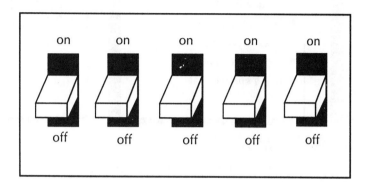

JUST TURN 'EM ALL OFF, WILL YA?

TEACHING NOTES
★★★★

Mega Nightmares

NCTM Standards
- Problem Solving
- Reasoning
- Number Theory
- Computation and Estimation
- Patterns and Functions
- Algebra

Possible Strategies
- Make a chart
- Look for a pattern
- Draw a picture
- Guess and check
- Use a spreadsheet

Suggested Materials
- Lined and unlined paper
- Calculator
- Computer spreadsheet

What to suggest if students are stuck

Draw a picture of the spiders. Draw circles for the bodies and add 3 or 8 legs on them. Draw enough to get close to 140 legs. If you end up too high or too low, trade some male (3 legs) and female (8 legs) flies until the total is 140 legs. Try this again to find another solution.

Make a chart as shown. Guess numbers of male and female flies until you get 140 legs. Look for patterns in the chart to help determine other combinations that will also give 140 legs.

Female (8)	Male (3)	Total
11	18	142
15	6	138

Make this chart on a spreadsheet. Fill in a formula for computing the total number of legs. Make guesses in an organized way so that you can see a pattern in the chart. Use the pattern to determine other solutions.

Complete solution

There are six combinations of male and female Mega-Flies. See the chart for the list.

Female (8)	Male (3)	Total
1	44	140
2	41	139
3	38	138
4	36	140
5	33	139
6	30	138
7	28	140
8	25	139
9	22	138
10	20	140
11	17	139
12	14	138
13	12	140
14	9	139
15	6	138
16	4	140
17	1	139

Notice the pattern. After the first combination of 140, each time 3 more females are added, 8 males are removed and the total number of legs remains 140.

Mega Nightmares

I shouldn't have watched that horror movie last night on TV. It gave me the strangest nightmare. I dreamed I was trapped on a planet of giant insects with Mega-Flies as big as elephants! I thought it was weird that the female Mega-Flies had 8 legs, and the male Mega-Flies only had 3 legs. In my dream I was caught in the web of a Mega-Spider who would not let me go unless I could solve his problem: How many Mega-Flies would he need to catch if he eats 140 Mega-Fly legs each day? He wants to know *all* the possibilities! What are they? _____

_____

_____

TEACHING NOTES
★★★★★

Read My Mind

NCTM Standards
- Problem Solving
- Reasoning
- Number Theory
- Computation and Estimation

Possible Strategies
- Use logical reasoning
- Eliminate possibilities
- Make a list

Suggested Materials
- Lined and unlined paper
- Calculator

What to suggest if students are stuck

Start a list of all the numbers between 225 (15^2) and 999 (largest three-digit number) that are odd and multiples of three. See which ones have a product of digits equal to 24. Look for a pattern in the numbers you find which might help you find the others without finishing the entire list.

Make a list of the factors of 24. Eliminate the two-digit factors. Choose sets of these which multiply to 24 and arrange them in all possible ways to make three-digit numbers. Check to see which of these are odd and multiples of three.

Complete solution

There are five numbers which fit the description. They are 381, 813, 831, 243, 423.

The factors of 24 are 1, 2, 3, 4, 6, 8, 12, 24. Using only the single-digit numbers, 24 can be obtained in 3 ways: 1 x 4 x 6; 1 x 3 x 8; 2 x 3 x 4. Arranging these digits into all possible numbers gives the following list. The ones which fit the conditions are marked.

146	less than 225
164	less than 225
416	even
461	not divisible by 3
614	even
641	not divisible by 3
138	less than 225
183	less than 225
318	even
381	Works! ←
813	Works! ←
831	Works! ←
234	even
243	Works! ←
324	even
342	even
423	Works! ←
432	even

Name _____

Read My Mind

I am thinking of a three-digit number. It is an odd multiple of three, and the product of its digits is 24. It is larger than 15^2. What are all the numbers I could be thinking of? _____

_____

IF2508 Problem of the Week—Grade 6

TEACHING NOTES
★★★★

Nick, the Knight

NCTM Standards
- Problem Solving
- Reasoning
- Number Theory

Possible Strategies
- Draw a picture
- Make a list
- Eliminate possibilities

Suggested Materials
- Lined and unlined paper
- Calculator

What to suggest if students are stuck

Draw a rectangle to stand for the castle. Mark 12 doors and number them from 1 through 12. Choose one door as Nick's entrance. Count how many exit choices he has. Now use a different door. Keep going until all possibilities have been used.

Make a list of the entry doors. Next to each, write the possible exit doors according to the wizard's rule. Continue until all possible combinations are recorded.

Make a list of all the possible combinations of entrance and exit doors without regard to the wizard's rule. Now cross out any which violate a rule. How many ways are left?

Complete solution

Nick has 35 ways to enter and exit the castle safely.

Door	Exits
12	6, 4, 3, 2, 1
11	1
10	5, 2, 1
9	3, 1
8	4, 2, 1
7	1
6	12, 3, 2, 1
5	10, 1
4	12, 8, 2, 1
3	12, 9, 6, 1
2	12, 10, 8, 6, 4, 1

Name _____

Nick, the Knight

Nick, the Knight, came upon an ancient castle inhabited by a very strange wizard. The castle has 12 huge doors, each guarded by a fierce dragon and numbered from 1 through 12. The wizard has a strict rule about the use of the doors. Knights may enter through any door except number 1. They must take note of the number of the door as they enter, because they are only permitted to leave through a door whose number is a factor or a multiple of the number of the entry door. Knights may not exit through the same door they entered. If a knight tries to leave through the wrong door, the dragons are to throw him into the moat with the crocodiles. In how many ways can Nick safely enter and exit this castle?

_____

I'LL TAKE DOOR NUMBER FOUR, WIZ!

Teaching Notes
★★★★★

Picnic Patterns

NCTM Standards	Possible Strategies	Suggested Materials
• Problem Solving • Reasoning • Geometry • Measurement	• Draw a picture • Act it out • Guess and check	• Lined and unlined paper • Calculator • Graph paper • Scissors

What to suggest if students are stuck

Draw the tablecloth on graph paper. Make a cut which follows the grid of the tablecloth. Check to see whether the pieces you formed are congruent. Check to see whether they can be rearranged to form a 2 x 15 rectangle.

Draw the tablecloth on graph paper. Cut the tablecloth into several pieces so that you can reform it to the size of the table. Take these small cut pieces and see how you might form them into two congruent pieces. Now go back to the original tablecloth and try to make a cut to form these two congruent pieces.

Complete solution

Cut the tablecloth and rearrange as shown.

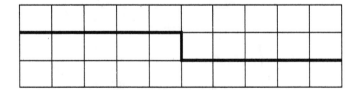

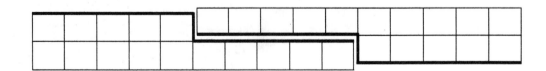

Picnic Patterns

Raakel and Marissa went on a picnic, but when they reached the park, they found that the picnic table was an unusual size. It was a rectangle 2 feet wide and 15 feet long. The red checkered tablecloth they brought was 3 feet wide and 10 feet long. They realized that the area was the same so they wanted to efficiently cut and piece together the tablecloth to fit the table. How could they cut the tablecloth along the checkerboard lines into two congruent pieces which could be rearranged to fit the table? _____

_____

_____

SOLVING THIS PROBLEM IS NO PICNIC!

TEACHING NOTES
★ ★ ★ ★

A Very Old Problem

NCTM Standards
- Problem Solving
- Reasoning
- Number Theory
- Computation and Estimation
- Algebra

Possible Strategies
- Use logical reasoning
- Make a chart
- Guess and check
- Look for a pattern

Suggested Materials
- Lined and unlined paper
- Calculator

What to suggest if students are stuck

Start by thinking about how pages in a book are set up. The pages have even numbers on the left and odd numbers on the right. If a book is open, the page numbers will follow one after another. Choose two consecutive numbers (even then odd). Multiply them and see how close this answer is to the target. Adjust your guess and try again.

Since the final digit must be a 2, determine the possible ones digits that could be used to produce a product with a 2 in the ones place. Also consider the magnitude of the target number. Use this to determine in which decade to begin guessing.

Make a chart to keep track of guesses. Look for patterns in the chart to help get to the target.

Left Page	Right Page	Product
80	81	6,480
82	83	6,806
84	85	7,140

Complete solution

The book is opened to pages 96 and 97.

Left Page	Right Page	Product
80	81	6,480
82	83	6,806
84	85	7,140
86	87	7,482
88	89	7,832
90	91	8,190
92	93	8,556
94	95	8,930
96	97	9,312

A Very Old Problem

An ancient manuscript is on display in a museum case. To what pages is the manuscript open if the product of the page numbers is 9,312? _____

_____

I'M GLAD I'M ANCIENT AND DON'T HAVE TO FIGURE THIS ONE OUT!

TEACHING NOTES
★ ★ ★ ★ ★
Mr. Y. B. Stingy's Estate

NCTM Standards
- Problem Solving
- Reasoning
- Number Relationships
- Computation and Estimation
- Algebra

Possible Strategies
- Make a chart
- Work backwards
- Guess and check

Suggested Materials
- Lined and unlined paper
- Calculator

What to suggest if students are stuck

Guess how much money he might have had. Work out the whole scenario using this value. If it does not work, adjust your guess and try again. Use each previous guess to help determine the next one.

Make a chart listing each person and the amount they were given, if known. Work backwards from the charity to determine how much each person was given. Add these figures to get the total value of the estate.

Wife		Half of Total
Son	$50,000	
Caddy		Half of Remainder
Iguana		Half of Remainder
Charity	$8,000	
Total	????	

Complete solution

His estate was worth $164,000.

Wife	$82,000	Half of Total
Son	$50,000	
Caddy	$16,000	Half of Remainder
Iguana	$8,000	Half of Remainder
Charity	$8,000	
Total	$164,000	

Mr. Y. B. Stingy's Estate

After Mr. Stingy died, his lawyer read the will to his family. He left half of his estate to his wife and $50,000 to his son. The remaining fortune was to be split in this way: half of what remained went to his caddy, half of what remained after that was set aside for the care of his pet iguana, and the remaining $8,000 went to his favorite charity. What was the value of Mr. Stingy's estate? _____

_____

TEACHING NOTES
★★★★

Cafeteria Combos

NCTM Standards
- Problem Solving
- Reasoning
- Computation and Estimation
- Patterns and Functions
- Probability

Possible Strategies
- Act it out
- Make a list
- Look for a pattern

Suggested Materials
- Lined and unlined paper
- Calculator

What to suggest if students are stuck

Write the names of the menu choices on slips of paper. Arrange these to create meals. Do this in a systematic way to make certain you have all of them.

Make a list of the possible meals. Start with EPP (eggplant pot pie) and BS (brussel sprouts). Put these together with all the dessert choices. Now use EPP with spinach salad and combine these with all the dessert choices. Continue in this way until you have all the possible combinations.

Look for patterns in the list above to allow you to predict the total number of meals.

Complete solution

There are 24 meal choices.

Main Dish	Side Dish	Dessert
EPP	BS	CC
EPP	BS	SP
EPP	SS	CC
EPP	SS	SP
EPP	MS	CC
EPP	MS	SP
EPP	SQ	CC
EPP	SQ	SP

This list of eight side dish/dessert combinations will be repeated with zucchini soufflé and with soybean burgers as the main dish (8 x 3 = 24 combinations).

Name _____

Cafeteria Combos

In my school cafeteria, Monday is vegetarian day. I can choose eggplant pot pie, zucchini soufflé, or soybean burgers for my main dish. The side dishes offered are brussel sprouts, spinach salad, mango slices, or squash. Luckily, the dessert choices are pretty good: chocolate cake or strawberry pie. How many different meal choices are there if each meal must consist of one main dish, one side dish, and a dessert? _____

_____

TEACHING NOTES
★★★★★
Pocketful of Change

NCTM Standards
- Problem Solving
- Reasoning
- Computation and Estimation

Possible Strategies
- Guess and check
- Make a list
- Eliminate possibilities
- Act it out

Suggested Materials
- Lined and unlined paper
- Calculator
- Play money

What to suggest if students are stuck

Take out 12 play coins. Find the total value. Trade coins until the value is exactly $1.00. Do more trading to find other combinations.

Make a chart as shown. Guess a combination of 12 coins. Find the total value. Adjust your guess and try again. Do this in a systematic way to ensure you have found all possibilities.

Nickels	Dimes	Quarters	Total Value
9	2	1	$0.90
8	3	1	$0.95

Start with a combination of coins that equals $1.00, no matter how many coins it takes. Trade coins for ones of equal value until the number of coins is 12.

Nickels	Dimes	Quarters	Total Value
	10		$1.00
2	9	0	$1.00

Complete solution

There are three possible combinations: 4 nickels and 8 dimes; 10 nickels and 2 quarters; 7 nickels, 4 dimes, and 1 quarter.

Nickels	Dimes	Quarters	Total Value
0	10	0	$1.00
2	9	0	$1.00
4	8	0	$1.00
20	0	0	$1.00
15	0	1	$1.00
10	0	2	$1.00
0	0	4	$1.00
1	2	3	$1.00
2	4	2	$1.00
3	6	1	$1.00
5	5	1	$1.00
7	4	1	$1.00

Pocketful of Change

I have exactly 12 coins in my pocket worth exactly $1.00. I might have nickels, dimes, and/or quarters. What combinations of coins might I have? Find all the possibilities. _____

_____

_____

TEACHING NOTES
★ ★ ★ ★ ★

Which Flavor?

NCTM Standards
- Problem Solving
- Reasoning
- Computation and Estimation

Possible Strategies
- Use logical reasoning
- Draw a picture

Suggested Materials
- Lined and unlined paper
- Calculator

What to suggest if students are stuck

List the information given and account for the overlapping data by subtracting the appropriate amounts from the list. For example, since 60 said "yes" to both, they were counted as part of the 80 who said "yes" to the first question and part of the 70 who said "yes" to the second question. Subtract this overlap. Find the total of the adjusted values.

Make a Venn diagram as shown. Fill in the information given. Account for the overlapping information in the diagram. Find the total.

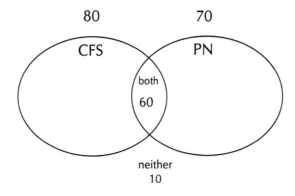

Complete solution

There were 100 students surveyed.

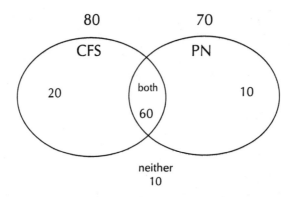

Which Flavor?

A group of middle school students completed the survey shown below.

Do you like Cappuccino Fudge Swirl Ice Cream? ____ yes ____ no

Do you like Pistachio Nut Ice Cream? ____ yes ____ no

When the results were tallied, it turned out that 80 answered "yes" to the first question, 70 answered "yes" to the second question, 60 responded "yes" to both questions, and 10 said "no" to both flavors. How many students were surveyed? _____

TEACHING NOTES
★★★★
Fashion Fun

NCTM Standards
- Problem Solving
- Reasoning
- Computation and Estimation
- Patterns and Functions

Possible Strategies
- Solve a simpler problem
- Look for a pattern
- Make a table
- Act it out
- Draw a picture

Suggested Materials
- Lined and unlined paper
- Calculator

What to suggest if students are stuck

Take out 18 counters or slips of paper to stand for the 18 socks. Arrange these to form all possible combinations. Do this in an organized way so that you are certain to find all of them.

Make a chart like this one to show how each sock can be paired. When the list is complete, find the total.

Sock	Number of Partners
1	17
2	16
3	15

Solve a simpler problem. Find out how many ways to pair the socks if she has 2, 3, 4, etc. Look for a pattern. Use this pattern to find the total.

Number of Socks Owned	Number of Pairs
2	1
3	3
4	6

Complete solution

There are 153 sock pairs that can be formed with 18 different socks.

Number of Socks Owned	Number of Pairs
2	1
3	3
4	6
5	10
6	15
7	21
8	28
9	36
10	45
11	55
12	66
13	78
14	91
15	105
16	120
17	136
18	153

+2
+3
+4

Notice the pattern. Each time the number of pairs increases by the next larger number.

Fashion Fun

Everyone thought that Martha Mathy was trying to start a new fashion trend when she started wearing socks that did not match. Her "look" started to catch on, and pretty soon all the kids at her school were wearing mixed-up socks, too. Rita Writer, a reporter for the school paper, interviewed Martha about the new sock trend. "What gave you the idea to wear mismatched socks?" Rita asked.

"It's simple mathematics," Martha replied. "You see, I have 18 socks at home, but no two are the same. With just these 18 socks, I can create over 100 unique pairs of mismatched socks." Rita found this hard to believe, so she checked it out. Was Martha correct?

Exactly how many sock pair combinations does Martha have? _____

SOCK IT TO ME!

TEACHING NOTES
★★★★★
Bean Bags

NCTM Standards
- Problem Solving
- Reasoning
- Computation and Estimation
- Algebra

Possible Strategies
- Make a chart
- Use logical reasoning
- Use a spreadsheet

Suggested Materials
- Lined and unlined paper
- Calculator
- Computer spreadsheet

What to suggest if students are stuck

Make a chart as shown below. Investigate combinations that total at least 17 pounds.

3-Pound Bags	5-Pound Bags	Total Pounds	Total Cost
6	0	18	$6.90
5	1	20	$7.38
2	3	21	$7.19

Use logical reasoning. Determine the unit cost of each type of bag. Try combinations which use more of the size which is cheaper per pound.

Make the chart above on a spreadsheet. Type the appropriate formula to find the total pounds and total cost. Enter numbers of bags of each size and look for the combination which is the cheapest for at least 17 pounds.

Complete solution

The cheapest way to get at least 17 pounds is to purchase one 3-pound bag and three 5-pound bags for $6.04.

3-Pound Bags	5-Pound Bags	Total Pounds	Total Cost
6	0	18	$6.90
5	1	20	$7.38
4	1	17	$6.23
3	2	19	$6.71
2	3	21	$7.19
1	3	18	$6.04
0	4	20	$6.52

Bean Bags

Lima beans come in 3-pound and 5-pound bags which cost $1.15 and $1.63 respectively. How many of each should you buy to have at least 17 pounds of lima beans at the lowest cost?

_____

_____

WHO THE HECK NEEDS SEVENTEEN POUNDS OF LIMA BEANS?

TEACHING NOTES
★★★★★
Basketball Scores

NCTM Standards
- Problem Solving
- Reasoning
- Computation and Estimation
- Algebra

Possible Strategies
- Make a table
- Guess and check

Suggested Materials
- Lined and unlined paper
- Calculator

What to suggest if students are stuck

Make a chart with three columns, one for each boy. Guess how many points Harold might have made. Determine how many points Isaac and Jacob would have made to make the totals work. Check your guess by using the last clue. If this does not work, adjust your guess and try again.

Start by listing all the combinations that add up to 14. This gives all the possible ways Isaac and Jacob might have scored points. For each combination in this list, see what score Harold might have gotten by subtracting Isaac's score from 19. If Harold's and Jacob's points add up to Isaac's score, this is the solution. If not, try the next pair with a sum of 14.

Complete solution

Harold made 8 points, Isaac made 11 points, and Jacob made 3 points.

Harold	Isaac	Jacob	
10	9	5	10 + 5 ≠ 9
7	12	2	7 + 2 ≠ 12
8	11	3	8 + 3 = 11

Basketball Scores

In a basketball game, Harold and Isaac scored a total of 19 points. Isaac and Jacob scored a total of 14 points. Isaac scored as many points as Harold and Jacob together. How many points did each player score? _____

AIR HAROLD!

TEACHING NOTES
★★★★★

Share and Share Alike

NCTM Standards
- Problem Solving
- Reasoning
- Number Relationships
- Computation and Estimation

Possible Strategies
- Draw a picture
- Guess and check
- Make a chart
- Act it out

Suggested Materials
- Lined and unlined paper
- Calculator
- Play money
- Counters

What to suggest if students are stuck

Take out counters to stand for cookies and play money worth $2.16. Act out the situation. Guess a "price" for each cookie and have Celeste pay each of the other two girls accordingly. If this price does not work fairly, guess another one.

Draw a picture of the cookies brought by each person. Mark the ones that should go to Celeste. For the payment to be fair, Brianna should be paid seven times as much as Allison. Make a chart to determine the amount for each girl.

A ◯◯◯◯◯◯◯ⓒ
B ◯◯◯◯◯◯◯◯ⓒⓒⓒⓒⓒⓒⓒ

Allison	Brianna	Total
$0.05	$0.35	$0.40
$0.10	$0.70	$0.80
$0.15	$1.05	$1.20

Determine the price of one cookie by dividing $2.16 by 8 since there are eight cookies to "buy." This gives the price of one cookie (which is what Allison gets). Brianna gets the rest of the money.

Complete solution

Allison should get $.27 and Brianna should get $1.89.

Allison	Brianna	Total
$0.05	$0.35	$0.40
$0.10	$0.70	$0.80
$0.15	$1.05	$1.20
$0.20	$1.40	$1.60
$0.25	$1.75	$2.00
$0.26	$1.82	$2.08
$0.27	$1.89	$2.16

Share and Share Alike

Allison, Brianna, and Celeste went on a hike. Allison brought 9 homemade cookies and Brianna brought 15 cookies she had made. Celeste forgot to bring treats, but she had $2.16. Allison and Brianna agreed that if the three were to share the cookies equally, then the two of them should divide Celeste's money equitably. Celeste agreed. What was the fair way to divide the money? _____

_____

'GUESS THIS MONEY IS COOKIE DOUGH!

TEACHING NOTES
★★★★
Triple Split

NCTM Standards
- Problem Solving
- Reasoning
- Computation and Estimation
- Geometry

Possible Strategies
- Draw a picture
- Make a model

Suggested Materials
- Lined and unlined paper
- Calculator
- Wooden cubes
- Graph paper

What to suggest if students are stuck

Build a "cake" that is 6 x 6 out of wooden cubes. Split it into three sections. Count cubes and frosted sides to see whether each section has the same number of each. If not, trade some cubes from one section to another.

Draw a 6 x 6 cake on graph paper. Label each square to show how many sides of that square are frosted. Determine the total number of frosted sides and divide this by 3 for the three girls. Use this information to help decide how to divide the cake.

Complete solution

To divide the cake evenly, each triplet must get 12 cake squares and 20 frosted sides. Many solutions are possible. One is shown.

3	2	2	2	2	3
2	1	1	1	1	2
2	1	1	1	1	2
2	1	1	1	1	2
2	1	1	1	1	2
3	2	2	2	2	3

Triple Split

For the triplets' birthday, Mom and Dad baked a 6 x 6 one-layer cake frosted on all sides and on the top. Gina, Tina, and Dina want to make certain that the cake is divided fairly among them. Show how the cake could be divided into three continuous pieces so that each triplet gets the same amount of cake and frosted sides as her sisters. _____

_____

WE LIKE TO HAVE OUR CAKE AND EAT IT, TOO!

TEACHING NOTES
★★★★★

Test Score Trouble

NCTM Standards
- Problem Solving
- Reasoning
- Computation and Estimation
- Statistics

Possible Strategies
- Guess and check
- Use logical reasoning

Suggested Materials
- Lined and unlined paper
- Calculator

What to suggest if students are stuck

There are four scores you can determine directly from the clues. You may need to review the definition of the words *median*, *mode*, and *range*. Record these scores in a list and leave the fifth one blank. Now, guess what the last test score might have been. Compute the mean using this score. If the mean comes out too high or too low, adjust your guess and compute the mean again.

Write the four known scores in a list with a blank space. To determine the missing score, remember that the mean must be 83 and use logic as shown below.

	100		83	83	58
Difference from the mean	+17	??	+0	+0	-25

Complete solution

The test scores are 100, 91, 83, 83, 58.

	100		83	83	58
Difference from the mean	+17	??	+0	+0	-25

The missing score must be 8 above the mean for the lower list to balance at zero (8 + 83 = 91).

Test Score Trouble

OOPS! Today I am supposed to tell my parents my grades on my last five math tests, but I forgot to bring the list home. I do remember these facts about my scores:

• I had one perfect test with a score of 100.

• The mean, median, and mode for my set of test scores turned out to be the same: 83.

• The range of my scores is 42.

What are my five test scores? _____

THIS PROBLEM IS MORE FUN THAN STEAMING BROCCOLI!

TEACHING NOTES
★★★★

Sixth Grade Round-Up

NCTM Standards
- Problem Solving
- Reasoning
- Computation and Estimation
- Patterns and Functions
- Algebra

Possible Strategies
- Make a chart
- Draw a picture
- Solve a simpler problem

Suggested Materials
- Lined and unlined paper
- Calculator

What to suggest if students are stuck

Start with a simpler problem. Pretend there were only 10 or 12 kids. Draw these situations and look for a pattern to predict the number opposite any number.

Make a chart listing student numbers and the number of the student across from him/her. Look for a pattern to predict the number directly across.

Complete solution

Monique's number is 303. Linus' number is 119. To find the number across from any number less than 180, add 180 to that number. To find the number across from any number greater than 180, subtract 180 from that number.

Number	Across
1	181
2	182
3	183
4	184
5	185
6	186
7	187
8	188
9	189
10	190
11	191
12	192
13	193
14	194
15	195

The number across from any number is half-way around the circle. Half this circle is 180 people, so to find the person across, add or subtract 180.

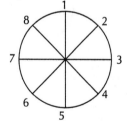
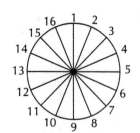

To find the number across from any number in a circle with n students, add n/2 to numbers between 1 and n/2. Subtract n/2 from numbers between n/2 and n.

Sixth Grade Round-Up

The entire sixth grade class gathered on the soccer field for a class picture. Since the photographer was not ready, the principal had all 360 students line up by height and form a circle. Helen was number 123, and her best friend, Monique, was directly opposite her in the circle. What number is Monique? Lucy was number 299, and her cousin, Linus, was directly across from her. What is Linus' number? Create a formula or rule that gives the number opposite any number in the circle. Write a rule that gives the number opposite any number no matter how many students are in a circle (assume there is always an even number of students). _____

TEACHING NOTES
★ ★ ★ ★ ★

Stocking the Student Store

NCTM Standards
- Problem Solving
- Reasoning
- Number Relationships
- Computation and Estimation
- Algebra

Possible Strategies
- Guess and check
- Make a chart
- Draw a picture

Suggested Materials
- Lined and unlined paper
- Calculator

What to suggest if students are stuck

Make a guess for the number of hats the store might have had. The number of T-shirts should be four times the number you guessed for hats. See whether the difference between these two numbers is 54. If not, make a new adjusted guess based on the results from the first guess.

Make a chart like this. Start with 1 hat and 55 T-shirts since there are 54 more T-shirts than hats. Divide the number of T-shirts by the number of hats to see whether you have four times as many T-shirts as hats. Now try 2 hats and 56 T-shirts and so on until you find a combination in which the number of T-shirts is four times the number of hats.

Hats	T-shirts	T-shirts ÷ Hats
1	55	55
2	56	28
3	57	19

Use letters to stand for hats and T-shirts (H = hat, T = T-shirt). Illustrate the condition of the problem that says there are four times as many T-shirts as hats by drawing rows like this: HTTTT
      HTTTT
Continue until there are 54 more Ts than Hs.

Complete solution

There were 18 hats and 72 T-shirts.

Hats	T-shirts	T-shirts – Hats
10	40	30
11	44	33
12	48	36
13	52	39
14	56	42
15	60	45
16	64	48
17	68	51
18	72	54

Stocking the Student Store

The student store sells school supplies, hats, and T-shirts with the school name printed on them. At the end of each month an inventory is taken to find out what needs to be ordered. The person who counted the hats and T-shirts cannot remember exactly how many of each there were, but he does remember two facts:

There were four times as many T-shirts as hats.
There were 54 more T-shirts than hats.

"No problem!" you tell him, "With this information I can figure out how many T-shirts and how many hats were in the store." What's the answer? _____

_____

NO PROBLEMO!

TEACHING NOTES
★★★★
Coin Shuffle

NCTM Standards
- Problem Solving
- Reasoning
- Patterns and Functions
- Geometry

Possible Strategies
- Act it out
- Make a list

Suggested Materials
- Lined and unlined paper
- Calculator
- Play coins or counters

What to suggest if students are stuck

Place coins or counters in the order given. Rearrange them according to the rules in the problem. Keep track of the moves you use by writing them on paper. Once you have found a solution, try it again and see whether you can do it in fewer moves.

Use a logical strategy like trying to get two like coins next to each other on each move. Try alternating moves to pair up nickels then dimes.

Complete solution

The change can be made in three moves:

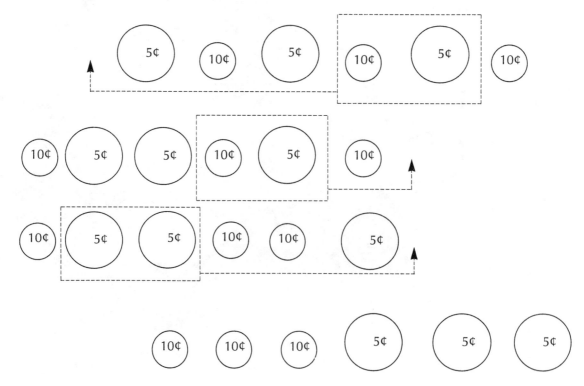

Name _____

Coin Shuffle

Place three dimes and three nickels on the table in the arrangement in the first row shown below. Your task is to move the coins so that all the dimes will end up on the left, and all the nickels will end up on the right as shown in the second row of coins you see below. You must slide the coins two at a time, without disturbing their order, and place them at either end of the row. Close the gap you created and move two more in the same way. Do this in the fewest number of moves possible. Show each move!

_____moves

Start like this:

Finish like this:

HEY PAL...
GOT TIME
FOR THIS
NICKEL
AND DIME
ASSIGNMENT?

TEACHING NOTES
★★★★★
Teacher Shortage

NCTM Standards
- Problem Solving
- Reasoning
- Number Relationships
- Computation and Estimation

Possible Strategies
- Draw a picture
- Guess and check
- Use logical reasoning

Suggested Materials
- Lined and unlined paper
- Calculator

What to suggest if students are stuck

Determine how many teachers the school has now. Since there are 26 students for every teacher, divide the number of students by 26 to find out how many teachers there are. Now make a guess as to how many new teachers might be added. See whether this number results in the ratio 19:1.

Draw a picture that shows the 26:1 ratio. Consider that each line represents a classroom with 26 students and 1 teacher.

```
SSSSSSSSSSSSSSSSSSSSSSSSSS        T
SSSSSSSSSSSSSSSSSSSSSSSSSS        T
SSSSSSSSSSSSSSSSSSSSSSSSSS        T
SSSSSSSSSSSSSSSSSSSSSSSSSS        T
        (95 classrooms)
```

If the ratio is reduced to 19:1, seven students must be removed from each class to form new classes of 19 students. Use the diagram and logic to determine how many new classes will be added.

Complete solution

Central Middle School needs 35 new teachers.

2,470 ÷ 26 = 95 teachers originally

2,470 ÷ 19 = 130 teachers needed to reduce the ratio

130 - 95 = 35 new teachers needed

Name _____

Teacher Shortage

Central Middle School has 2,470 students and the ratio of students to teachers is 26:1. How many new teachers are needed to reduce this ratio to 19:1? _____

COMMUNICATING QUITE CLEARLY IS THE CLASSIC CONUNDRUM!

WOULDN'T YOU AGREE?

TEACHING NOTES
★★★★★

Volleyball Team

NCTM Standards
- Problem Solving
- Reasoning
- Computation and Estimation
- Patterns and Functions
- Probability

Possible Strategies
- Act it out
- Make a list
- Look for a pattern

Suggested Materials
- Lined and unlined paper
- Calculator
- Counters

What to suggest if students are stuck

Take out 12 counters and mark them A–L to stand for the 12 girls. Arrange them in pairs and keep track of all the ways you find. Do this in a systematic way and look for a pattern. The chance that Heather and Louisa will both be chosen is one out of the total number of possible pairings.

Make a list of all the possible pairings using a systematic list. Start with Annie. Pair her with all the other girls. Now do the same for Becky, etc. Look for a pattern in this list so that you do not have to list all combinations. Use this to determine the probability that Heather and Louisa will be chosen together.

Complete solution

There is a 1 in 66 chance that Heather and Louisa will be chosen together.

AB	BC	CD	DE	EF	FG	GH	HI	IJ	JK	KL
AC	BD	CE	DF	EG	FH	GI	HJ	IK	JL	
AD	BE	CF	DG	EH	FI	GJ	HK	IL		
AE	BF	CG	DH	EI	FJ	GK	**HL**			
AF	BG	CH	DI	EJ	FK	GL				
AG	BH	CI	DJ	EK	FL					
AH	BI	CJ	DK	EL						
AI	BJ	CK	DL							
AJ	BK	CL								
AK	BL									
AL										
11	**10**	**9**	**8**	**7**	**6**	**5**	**4**	**3**	**2**	**1**

There is one fewer pairing for each successive player, so the number of ways will be
$$11 + 10 + 9 + 8 + 7 + 6 + 5 + 4 + 3 + 2 + 1 = 66.$$
One of these ways has Heather with Louisa.

Volleyball Team

The list below names the 12 athletes who are trying out for two openings on the girls' volleyball team. Each of the girls on the list is an excellent player, so Coach Netter decided to use a random method for choosing the two girls who will make the team. Heather and Louisa are best friends and would love to be on the team together. What are the chances that Coach will choose both of them?_____

Volleyball Try-out List

Annie	Gloria
Becky	Heather
Carla	Ingrid
Dolores	Juanita
Evette	Kelly
Francine	Louisa

ONE POTATO, TWO POTATO, THREE...

TEACHING NOTES
★★★★
Triangle Trends

NCTM Standards
- Problem Solving
- Reasoning
- Geometry

Possible Strategies
- Act it out
- Draw a picture
- Look for a pattern

Suggested Materials
- Lined and unlined paper
- Calculator
- Triangular tiles
- Triangular grid paper

What to suggest if students are stuck

Use triangle tiles to form a shape. Cut this shape out of triangular grid paper. Now arrange the tiles in another way. Cut this one out. Continue doing this until you have found all the possibilities.

Start with a "basic" tile arrangement like a line. Take one triangle off the end and place it in all the other locations it could go around the shape. See which arrangements create new shapes.

Complete solution

There are three shapes that can be formed from four triangles.

There are four shapes that can be formed from five triangles.

There are 12 shapes that can be formed from six triangles.

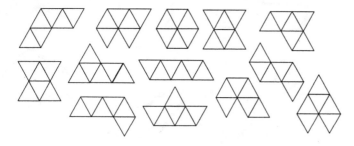

Triangle Trends

Tracy found a bunch of identical tiles in the shape of equilateral triangles. She began exploring ways to put triangles together to make different shapes. She followed these two rules when putting triangles together:

- always have full sides touch
- always have corners meet

She was really surprised to find that with two tiles, she could only form one

shape:

And with three tiles she could only form one shape:

Continue Tracy's investigation. How many noncongruent shapes can be made using four triangle tiles?_____ Using five triangle tiles? _____ Using six triangle tiles? _____ Record using a picture.

THIS TRIANGLE TREND IS TRULY TAXING!

TEACHING NOTES
★★★★
And the Winner Is . . .

NCTM Standards
- Problem Solving
- Reasoning
- Computation and Estimation
- Patterns and Functions
- Probability

Possible Strategies
- Make a list
- Act it out
- Look for a pattern
- Solve a simpler problem

Suggested Materials
- Lined and unlined paper
- Calculator
- Graph paper
- Counters

What to suggest if students are stuck

Take out 15 counters to represent the people in the drawing. Mark one to represent "you." Arrange the counters to show the winner of the trip and the winner of movie passes and all the losers. Keep track of all the arrangements. Do this in a systematic way so that you can be certain you have found all of them.

Solve a simpler problem. If only two people entered the drawing, how many ways would there be to assign the prizes? What if three people entered? Continue and look for a pattern.

Make a list of all the ways the prizes could be assigned as shown. Let A–O stand for the 15 people in the drawing. The first letter listed is the winner of the trip; the second is the winner of the movie passes. Let's say you are A; determine how many ways include you as a winner.

AB	BA	CA
AC	BC	CB
AD	BD	CD
AE	BE	CE
AF	BF	CF
AG	BG	CG
AH	BH	CH
AI	BI	CI
AJ	BJ	CJ
AK	BK	CK
AL	BL	CL

Complete solution

There are 210 ways the prizes can be awarded. Twenty-eight of them include me.

1	AB	BA	CA
2	AC	BC	CB
3	AD	BD	CD
4	AE	BE	CE
5	AF	BF	CF
6	AG	BG	CG
7	AH	BH	CH
8	AI	BI	CI
9	AJ	BJ	CJ
10	AK	BK	CK
11	AL	BL	CL
12	AM	BM	CM
13	AN	BN	CN
14	AO	BO	CO

Notice that there are 14 ways to assign the second prize if A gets the first prize. If this chart were completed, it would have 15 columns (A–O) with 14 in each column or 210 ways to assign the prizes. If I am A, there are 14 ways for me to win the trip (first column) and 14 ways for me to win the movie passes (A occurs once in each of the other columns). So 28 of the 210 ways include me as a winner.

And the Winner Is. . .

I entered a drawing for two fabulous prizes: a trip to Disneyland or a year's supply of movie passes. Fourteen other people also entered the drawing.

How many ways can the prizes be awarded? _____

How many of them include me? _____

WOULDN'T I JUST LOOK GROOVY IN MOUSE EARS?

TEACHING NOTES
★★★★★
The Ten-Dollar Bargains

NCTM Standards
- Problem Solving
- Reasoning
- Computation and Estimation
- Patterns and Functions

Possible Strategies
- Guess and check
- Make a chart
- Look for a pattern
- Act it out
- Work backwards

Suggested Materials
- Lined and unlined paper
- Calculator
- Play money

What to suggest if students are stuck

Guess how much money you might have had to start. Take this out in play money. Act out the scenario and see how much money is left at the end. If it does not work out, make a new guess and try again.

Make a chart to keep track of the guesses. Look for a pattern to help determine the original amount.

Item	Have	Get	Spend	Left
hat	$9.00	$9.00	$10.00	$8.00
shoes	$8.00	$8.00	$10.00	$6.00
umbrella	$6.00	$6.00	$10.00	$2.00

Work backwards from the purchase of the umbrella. Since you had nothing left after buying the umbrella, which cost $10, you must have had $5 and been given $5. This means you must have had $5 left after buying the shoes. You spent $10 making a total of $15 after Mike gave you some money. How much would you have had, and how much would he have given you? Use this logic one more time to determine how much you had before you bought the hat.

Complete solution

I had $8.75 to start.

Item	Have	Get	Spend	Left
hat	$9.00	$9.00	$10.00	$8.00
shoes	$8.00	$8.00	$10.00	$6.00
umbrella	$6.00	$6.00	$10.00	$2.00
hat	$6.00	$6.00	$10.00	$2.00
shoes	$2.00	$2.00	$10.00	not enough
umbrella				
hat	$8.00	$8.00	$10.00	$6.00
shoes	$6.00	$6.00	$10.00	$2.00
umbrella	$2.00	$2.00	$10.00	not enough
hat	$8.50	$8.50	$10.00	$7.00
shoes	$7.00	$7.00	$10.00	$4.00
umbrella	$4.00	$4.00	$10.00	not enough
hat	$8.75	$8.75	$10.00	$7.50
shoes	$7.50	$7.50	$10.00	$5.00
umbrella	$5.00	$5.00	$10.00	$0.00

The Ten-Dollar Bargains

I love a bargain! My friend and I went to the department store to buy a new hat. The hat I wanted cost $10. I did not have that much money in my pocket, so I made this proposal to my good and generous friend, Moneybags Mike: "I have between $5 and $10 in my pocket. If you will loan me as much money as I now have, I will have enough money to buy that $10 hat and have some money left over." My good and generous friend agreed and I bought the hat. Then I saw a pair of shoes I could not live without, but I did not have enough money. I assured my generous friend, Moneybags Mike, that I would repay him soon if he would loan me the amount of money equal to what I now had in my pocket to buy the $10 pair of shoes. He agreed. We did the same procedure again for a $10 umbrella. I was then out of money. How much money did I have when I walked into the department store? (no sales tax!) _____

TEACHING NOTES
★ ★ ★ ★

I Need That Grade

NCTM Standards
- Problem Solving
- Reasoning
- Number Relationships
- Computation and Estimation
- Algebra

Possible Strategies
- Guess and check
- Use logical reasoning
- Use a spreadsheet

Suggested Materials
- Lined and unlined paper
- Calculator
- Computer spreadsheet

What to suggest if students are stuck

Compute the grade assuming he gets 0 of the remaining 90 points. Compute his grade assuming he gets all 90 of the remaining 90 points. Using these extremes, guess and test some numbers of points and see what his grade will be.

Use the total number of points for the quarter (880 + 90 = 970). Find 69.5% of this amount, 79.5%, and 89.5%. This will tell you how many points are needed for each desired grade.

Make a chart to determine the percent that will result from any number of points earned. Keep going until 80% and 90% are reached.

If I get	my total will be	out of	for _____% (rounded)
0	730	970	75%
1	731	970	75%
2	732	970	75%
3	733	970	76%

Make this chart on a spreadsheet. Type the appropriate formulas in the cells for finding his total and for the percent. Find the number of points needed for each grade.

Complete solution

No points are needed to make a C grade.
42 points are needed to make a B grade.
It is impossible to make an A.

If I get	my total will be	out of	for _____% (rounded)
0	730	970	75%
38	768	970	79%
39	769	970	79%
40	770	970	79%
41	771	970	79%
42	772	970	80%
90	820	970	85%

I Need That Grade

It is almost the end of the grading period. I have 730 out of 880 points so far in my math class which means I currently have a B (83%). There are 90 points remaining before grades come out. My teacher rounds each student's score to the nearest percent. What is the fewest number of points I need to get and end up with a grade of   C (at least 70%)? _____

B (at least 80%)? _____

A (at least 90%)? _____

TEACHING NOTES
★★★★★

Pencil Packages

NCTM Standards
- Problem Solving
- Reasoning
- Number Theory
- Patterns and Functions

Possible Strategies
- Act it out
- Make a list
- Use logical reasoning
- Look for a pattern

Suggested Materials
- Lined and unlined paper
- Calculator
- Counters

What to suggest if students are stuck

Take out counters in two colors. Let one color stand for the three-packs and the other for the eight-packs. Use these to experiment with different combinations to make as many totals as you can. Record these.

Make a list of the numbers from 1 to 50 (or a number of your choosing). Fill in the combinations you can think of for some of the numbers. For example, all the multiples of 3 can be made using three-packs. All the multiples of 8 can be found using eight-packs. Now try combinations of 3s and 8s. Find that total in your list. For example 2 eight-packs and 3 three-packs make 25. Write this on the line for 25. Continue until you have found all possible totals. Make a generalization about finding numbers higher than 50.

Make the list described above, but work systematically. First fill in all multiples of 3 and 8. Next take one 3 with one 8 (11) and continually add 3s to this. Next, go back to 11 and continually add 8s. Take a new starting point like two 3s and continue in this way.

Complete solution

The numbers which are impossible are 1, 2, 4, 5, 7, 10, 13. All other numbers are possible.

Packs of 3	Packs of 8	Total
1	0	3
2	0	6
0	1	8
3	0	9
1	1	11
4	0	12
2	1	14
5	0	15
0	2	16
3	1	17
6	0	18
1	2	19
4	1	20
7	0	21
2	2	22
5	1	23
8	0	24
3	2	25
6	1	26
9	0	27

Notice the pattern that has been established. Every third number can be obtained by using one more pack of 3. Between each of these (marked with arrows) is a line using one pack of 8 followed by a line using two packs of 8.

The continuation of this pattern ensures that all remaining numbers will be possible.

Pencil Packages

At the student store pencils are sold in packs of three or packs of eight. Without opening any packages, which numbers of pencils is it possible to buy? _____ Which numbers are impossible? _____

I WONDER HOW MANY PENCILS I'LL USE THIS YEAR!

TEACHING NOTES
★★★★★

Tables for Six . . . or Eight

NCTM Standards
- Problem Solving
- Reasoning
- Computation and Estimation
- Patterns and Functions
- Algebra
- Geometry

Possible Strategies
- Guess and check
- Make a chart
- Look for a pattern
- Draw a picture
- Use a spreadsheet

Suggested Materials
- Lined and unlined paper
- Calculator
- Computer spreadsheet

What to suggest if students are stuck

Draw a picture of 35 tables. Write a 6 or 8 inside each one to show how many seats are at each. Total the numbers and see whether they equal 236. If not, adjust and guess again.

Make a chart as shown. Guess a number of each type of table so that the total number of tables is 236. Guess in a systematic way and look for a pattern in the chart.

Hexagons	Octagons	Total Tables	Total Seats
10	25	35	260
11	24	35	258

Make this table on a spreadsheet. Fill in the appropriate formulas for finding the total number of tables and the total number of seats. Look for the combination that fits the conditions.

Complete solution

There are 22 hexagon tables and 13 octagon tables.

Hexagons	Octagons	Total Tables	Total Seats
10	25	35	260
11	24	35	258
12	23	35	256
13	22	35	254
14	21	35	252
22	13	35	236

Notice that every time you trade an octagon table for a hexagon table, two fewer seats result. To reach 236, 252 must be reduced by 16; this means adding 8 hexagons and eliminating 8 octagons.

Tables for Six . . . or Eight

The library in Geotown has a large room with enough tables and chairs to seat 236 people. Some of the tables are in the shape of a hexagon and seat six people each. The rest of the tables are octagonal and seat eight people each. If there are 35 tables in the room, how many are hexagons and how many are octagons? _____

WOW! MANY PEOPLE IN GEOTOWN MUST USE THE LIBRARY!

One-centimeter Graph Paper

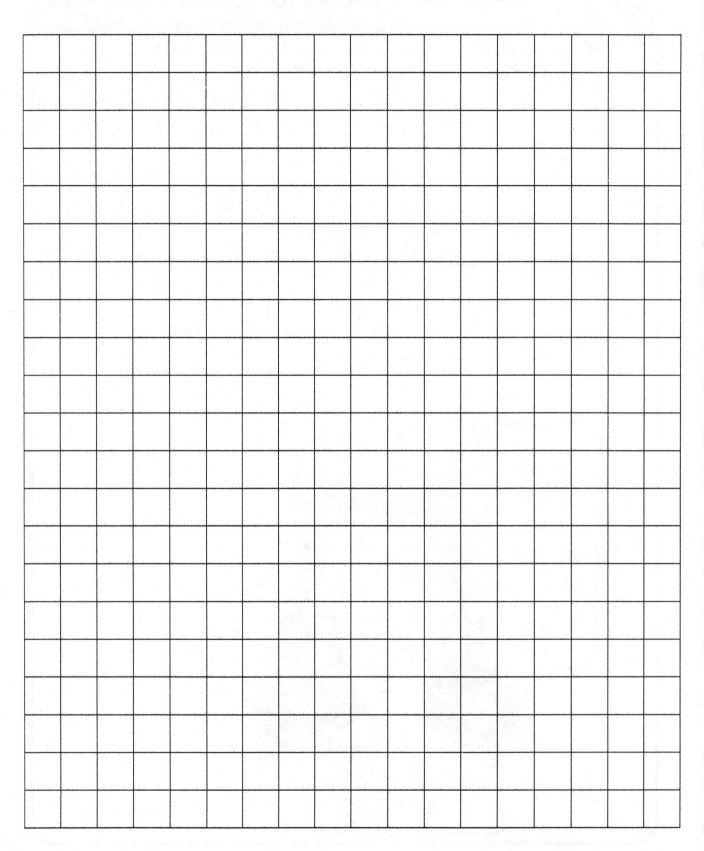

One-inch Graph Paper

Play Money

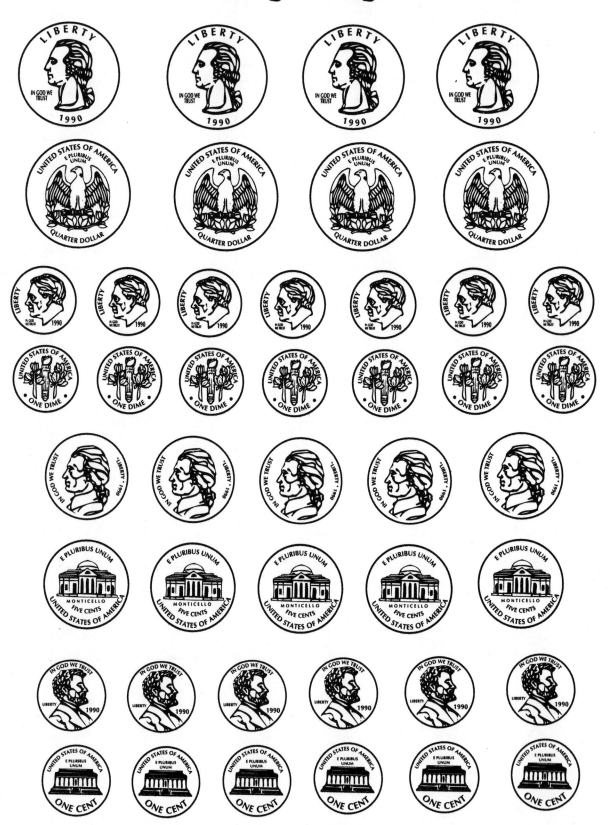

Triangular Grid Paper

Trapezoid Master

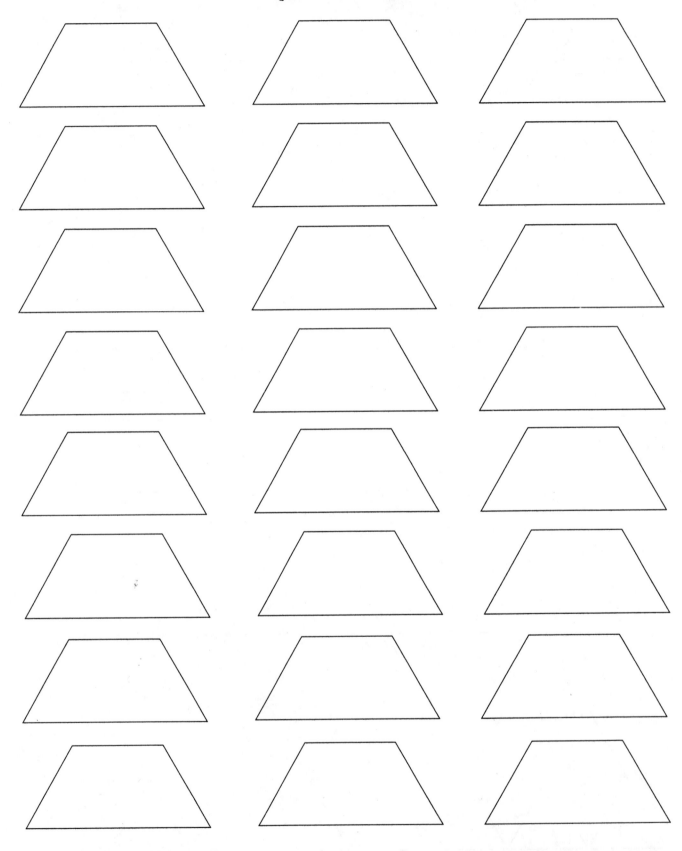